"20 TIPS FOR CRAFTING YOUR SUCCESS THROUGH A POSITIVE LEADERSHIP MINDSET"

A Comprehensive Guide To Shaping A Positive Leadership Mindset For Lasting Success In The Modern Business World"

Professor James Dorman

About Author

Professor James Dorman stands as the preeminent author, distinguished by a profound understanding of Leadership and Management, Health and Nutrition, Relationship dynamics, Personal development, and Bible Knowledge.

His works encapsulate a harmonious blend of high sensibility and deep knowledge, establishing him as the first-choice authority in these domains. With an innate ability to articulate complex concepts and a commitment to enlightening readers, Professor Dorman's writings transcend conventional boundaries, offering invaluable insights that resonate with individuals seeking guidance in leadership, holistic health, interpersonal dynamics, personal growth, and spiritual understanding.

A trailblazer in multifaceted wisdom, he leaves an indelible mark as a beacon of knowledge across diverse disciplines.

Book Review

Leadership And Management.
Career And Success.

With "Mindful Leadership," a guide that transcends conventional leadership paradigms, set off on a transforming adventure.

This book, which draws on "Navigating Challenges, Inspiring Teams," is an all-inclusive tool for developing a positive leadership mindset. Learn how to overcome obstacles, promote growth, and build resilience.

It offers practical advice for attaining long-term success in the ever-changing corporate environment of today, from developing a conscious approach to leadership to motivating colleagues. This book serves as a helpful compass for navigating complexity and cultivating an optimistic outlook that propels individuals and teams toward common goals.

Introduction

Welcome to the transformative pages of "Mindful Leadership: Crafting Your Success Through a Positive Leadership Mindset."

In the dynamic tapestry of today's business world, effective leadership transcends traditional paradigms. Drawing inspiration from the essence encapsulated in "Navigating Challenges, Inspiring Teams," this book is a compass for leaders seeking enduring success.

In this comprehensive guide, we embark on a journey that goes beyond conventional approaches, delving into the intricacies of shaping a positive leadership mindset.

The modern business world demands resilience and inspiration, and this book serves as a roadmap to cultivate just that.

From navigating challenges with mindfulness to inspiring teams towards collective growth, each chapter unfolds actionable insights for fostering lasting success.

The pages within are not just words; they are a reservoir of strategies to craft a positive mindset that navigates complexities with grace. It is an exploration of leadership that not only guides personal success but becomes the catalyst for elevating entire teams toward shared accomplishments.

As you delve into the principles within, may "Mindful Leadership" be your companion on the journey toward leadership excellence in the contemporary business landscape, where positivity becomes the cornerstone for enduring success.

Table Of Content

<u>Chapter One</u>

"Embracing Care In Initiative: An Outline For Progress"

In the unique scene of authority, embracing care arises as an extraordinary plan for unmatched achievement. At its center, care in administration typifies a purposeful and non-critical familiarity with the current second. By developing this mindfulness, pioneers can explore difficulties with increased clearness, settling on informed choices that resound with both the quick setting and long haul objectives.

A vital part of this plan lies in mindfulness. Pioneers who practice care take part in thoughtfulness, grasping their assets, shortcomings, and triggers. This mindfulness shapes a strong groundwork, permitting pioneers to interface with their groups and encourage a culture of receptiveness and trust genuinely.

Moreover, care mixes authority with compassionate correspondence. Pioneers receptive to the current second can really stand by listening to their colleagues, grasp different points of view, and answer with compassion. This establishes a steady climate, improving coordinated effort and generally speaking group execution.

Vital independent direction turns out to be more nuanced when directed by care. By moving toward difficulties with an unmistakable and centered mind, pioneers can perceive needs, evaluate dangers, and devise creative arrangements. This proactive and smart navigation is a sign of effective initiative.

All in all, the joining of care into initiative practices gives an exhaustive outline to progress. It enables pioneers to explore intricacies with flexibility, cultivate certifiable associations, and pursue vital choices that move the two people and associations towards supported greatness.

Key Idea; Viable procedures for incorporating care rehearses into your initiative methodology.

1. Daily Careful Rituals:
Start your day with brief care works out, like careful breathing or a short contemplation. This establishes an inspirational vibe and improves your concentration for the difficulties ahead.

2. Mindful Choice Making:
Integrate care into dynamic by pausing for a minute to stop, reflect, and think about different viewpoints. This assists in pursuing with welling educated and smart decisions.

3. Active Listening:
Practice careful tuning in during discussions. Completely participate in the current second, center around the speaker, and keep away from performing various tasks. This cultivates better comprehension and fortifies relational connections.

4. Mindful Communication:
Express yourself carefully, guaranteeing clearness and compassion in your correspondence. Careful

correspondence encourages a positive and steady workplace.

5. Mindful Breaks:

Energize short care breaks for you as well as your group over the course of the day. These breaks can incorporate extending works out, profound breathing, or a concise walk, advancing mental lucidity and lessening pressure.

6. Mindful Initiative Improvement Programs:

Incorporate care into authority preparing programs. Give assets and studios that enable pioneers with reasonable apparatuses for integrating care into their everyday schedules.

7. Mindful Delegation:

While designating undertakings, move toward it with care. Consider each colleague's assets and responsibility, guaranteeing a reasonable dissemination of obligations that line up with individual capacities.

8. Reflective Practices:

Energize normal reflection on initiative practices. Carefully survey your activities, gain from encounters, and adjust systems for constant improvement.

By meshing these commonsense procedures into your initiative methodology, you can efficiently incorporate care, cultivating a strong and centered authority style that adds to both individual and hierarchical achievement.

Chapter Two

"Tough Authority: Exploring Difficulties With Effortlessness And Certainty"

Strong authority remains as a relentless point of support despite difficulties, encapsulating the ability to explore difficulty with effortlessness and certainty. At its center, strength in administration relies on versatility, the capacity to appreciate people on a profound level, and a steady obligation to development.

A tough chief flourishes in the midst of vulnerability, seeing difficulties not as unrealistic snags but rather as any open doors for development and learning. This outlook takes into account spry direction, empowering pioneers to turn when important without failing to focus on all-encompassing objectives.

The ability to appreciate anyone on a deeper level structures the foundation of exploring difficulties with beauty. Strong pioneers are receptive to their feelings and those of their group, cultivating a steady climate. This compassionate methodology fabricates trust and attachment, fundamental components in defeating hindrances all in all.

Trust in versatile administration radiates from a profound comprehension of one's capacities and impediments. Pioneers who radiate certainty motivate trust and hopefulness inside their groups, making a culture where difficulties are met with an aggregate confidence in the capacity to survive.

Besides, cultivating strength includes constant self-reflection and a promise to individual and expert turn of events. Gaining from misfortunes, commending triumphs, and adjusting procedures add to a development situated initiative style.

Fundamentally, versatile initiative is a unique power that changes difficulties into open doors, exhibiting an immovable capacity to control through misfortune with beauty and certainty. This approach strengthens pioneers as well as develops a strong culture inside groups, moving associations toward supported outcome in a consistently advancing scene.

Key Idea; Bits of knowledge on building versatility to really deal with and beat administration challenges.

Building strength to really deal with and defeat initiative difficulties requires a diverse methodology that joins mindfulness, versatility, and a guarantee to ceaseless development. Here are key experiences to strengthen flexibility in administration:

1. Self-Mindfulness As A Foundation:
Versatile pioneers start by figuring out their assets, shortcomings, and profound triggers. This mindfulness gives a strong groundwork, permitting pioneers to answer as opposed to respond to difficulties, encouraging a quiet and estimated approach.

2. Agile Outlook And Adaptability:
Versatility flourishes in a dexterous attitude. Pioneers who embrace change and view difficulties

as any open doors for development are better prepared to explore complex circumstances. The capacity to adjust methodologies and turn when vital is pivotal for beating unforeseen snags.

3. Cultivate Close To home Intelligence:

Versatility is interlaced with the ability to understand anyone at their core. Pioneers who can perceive, comprehend, and deal with their feelings, as well as understand the feelings of others, establish a strong climate. This close to home mindfulness cultivates more grounded connections and successful cooperation during testing times.

4. Strategic Choice Making:

Tough pioneers pursue choices decisively, gauging choices and taking into account long haul suggestions. They stay zeroed in on all-encompassing objectives while being adaptable in their methodology. This essential independent direction is crucial for guiding through vulnerabilities and difficulties.

5. Continuous Learning And Adaptation:

Flexibility is a unique quality that blossoms with gaining from encounters. Pioneers focused on constant learning, both from victories and disappointments, are better prepared to refine their administration styles and adjust to developing difficulties.

6. Team Strengthening And Collaboration:

Building versatility reaches out past individual pioneers to include the whole group. Versatile pioneers engage their groups, cultivating a cooperative climate where different abilities add to imaginative critical thinking. Shared difficulties become shared triumphs.

7. Maintaining A Positive Outlook:

Strong pioneers keep an uplifting perspective even despite misfortune. This hopeful attitude spurs the group as well as ingrains certainty that difficulties can be survived. Uplifting feedback and festivity of little wins add to a versatile hierarchical culture.

8. Stress The board And Well-being:

Focusing on pressure the executives and individual prosperity is essential to building flexibility. Pioneers who perceive the significance of taking care of oneself can more readily endure the tensions of authority, guaranteeing supported adequacy over the long haul.

All in all, building strength in initiative is a continuous cycle that includes mindfulness, versatility, the capacity to understand people on a profound level, and a guarantee to constant learning. By exemplifying these standards, pioneers can successfully deal with and defeat difficulties, encouraging their self-awareness as well as the versatility of their groups and associations.

<u>Chapter Three</u>

"The Force Of Positive Authority: Rousing Groups For Aggregate Development"

The force of positive authority lies in its extraordinary capacity to rouse groups and drive aggregate development. Positive initiative is in excess of a mentality; a conscious methodology cultivates a hopeful culture, energizes cooperation, and develops a feeling of direction inside groups.

At its center, positive authority is infectious. Pioneers who ooze inspiration establish a climate where colleagues feel propelled, esteemed, and locked in. This, thus, improves efficiency and advancement, as people are bound to contribute their best when encircled by inspiration.

Rousing groups for aggregate development includes viable correspondence that accentuates qualities and accomplishments. Positive pioneers perceive and praise individual and group victories, supporting a culture of consistent improvement and versatility.

Besides, positive initiative sustains a common vision. Pioneers articulate a convincing reason that resounds with colleagues, encouraging a feeling of having a place and responsibility. At the point when people comprehend the meaning of their commitments to the bigger objective, it fills aggregate development.

The effect of positive administration stretches out past the working environment. It fabricates trust and encourages more grounded relational connections, making a steady air where difficulties are seen as any open doors for learning and improvement.

Basically, the force of positive initiative lies in its capacity to make a flourishing biological system where people are enlivened to arrive at their maximum capacity. By developing a positive culture, pioneers lift camaraderie as well as establish the groundwork for supported aggregate development and achievement.

Key Idea; Uncovering the effect of a positive initiative mentality in group motivation and achievement.

1. Cultivating Motivation:

A positive initiative outlook fills in as a strong inspiration for groups. Pioneers who ooze inspiration establish a climate where colleagues feel motivated to contribute their earnest attempts, encouraging an aggregate drive for progress.

2. Fostering A Cooperative Culture:

Energy in initiative advances a cooperative culture. Colleagues are urged to share thoughts, team up on projects, and impart straightforwardly. This comprehensive climate upgrades innovativeness and development, adding to the general progress of the group.

3. Building Resilience:

Positive pioneers ingrain strength inside their groups. When confronted with difficulties, a positive outlook supports an arrangements situated approach. Colleagues view misfortunes as transitory and as any open doors for development, developing a strong demeanor pivotal for long haul achievement.

4. Enhancing Group Cohesion:

A positive initiative outlook fortifies group union. By perceiving and commending individual and aggregate accomplishments, pioneers make a feeling of solidarity. This union lifts the general mood as well as lays out a strong starting point for conquering snags.

5. Creating A Culture Of Appreciation:

Positive pioneers underscore appreciation and acknowledgment. Recognizing the endeavors of colleagues cultivates a positive workplace, building up the possibility that every commitment is significant. This, thusly, improves work fulfillment and group responsibility.

6. Encouraging A Development Situated Mindset:

A positive initiative mentality empowers a development situated point of view. Pioneers center around fostering the qualities of people, giving chances to learning, and review difficulties as venturing stones for development. This attitude adds to ceaseless individual and group advancement.

7. Elevating Group Morale:

Energy straightforwardly affects camaraderie. At the point when pioneers keep a hopeful standpoint, it makes an expanding influence, impacting the general state of mind of the group. Raised resolve converts into expanded commitment, efficiency, and a more charming workplace.

8. Inspiring A Common Vision:

Positive pioneers move groups by articulating a convincing vision. Conveying a feeling of direction and shared objectives cultivates an aggregate personality, adjusting individual endeavors to the more extensive mission. This common vision turns into a main thrust for group achievement.

In outline, a positive initiative mentality significantly impacts group motivation and accomplishment by developing inspiration, cultivating cooperation, building strength, upgrading union, advancing appreciation, empowering development, raising spirit, and rousing a common vision. These components all in all add to a flourishing and fruitful group dynamic.

<u>Chapter Four</u>

"Careful Independent direction: A Critical To Powerful Initiative"

Careful dynamic stands as a foundation of compelling initiative, enveloping a purposeful and present-disapproved of way to deal with decisions that significantly influences hierarchical achievement. At its quintessence, this idea includes developing an uplifted consciousness of the current second, taking into account different viewpoints, and settling on choices with purposeful clearness.

Pioneers who focus on careful direction take part in an intelligent cycle that goes past the surface. They recognize and deal with their own inclinations and feelings, guaranteeing that decisions are made in light of a thorough comprehension of the circumstance. This mindfulness is critical for staying away from rash choices and encouraging a prudent initiative style.

Moreover, careful navigation includes a compassionate thought of others' perspectives. Pioneers who carve out opportunity to comprehend the worries and viewpoints of their colleagues make a comprehensive dynamic cycle. This fortifies connections as well as takes advantage of the aggregate insight of the group, prompting all the more balanced and powerful decisions.

The clearness acquired through careful direction is instrumental in exploring intricacies. Pioneers can focus on targets, evaluate gambles, and expect results with an engaged psyche. This essential methodology adds to authoritative versatility and flexibility even with difficulties.

Basically, careful navigation goes past a simple mental interaction; it incorporates the capacity to understand individuals on a profound level, mindfulness, and a smart thought of others. Pioneers who embrace this approach make a culture of deliberate and viable direction, driving their groups and associations toward supported achievement.

Key Idea; Investigating how a careful methodology improves decision-production for pioneers.

1. Increased Self-Awareness:

Careful dynamic starts with elevated mindfulness. Pioneers who practice care are receptive to their viewpoints, feelings, and inclinations, empowering them to settle on choices with their very own reasonable comprehension viewpoints and expected impacts.

2. Emotional Regulation:

Care outfits pioneers with the instruments to direct their feelings, forestalling hasty navigation driven by pressure or disappointment. This profound equilibrium takes into account more reasonable and thought about decisions.

3. Reduced Mental Biases:

Care helps pioneers perceive and relieve mental predispositions. By remaining present at the time, pioneers are better ready to recognize and challenge assumptions, prompting more genuine navigation.

4. Enhanced Concentration And Clarity:

A careful methodology encourages fixation and mental lucidity. Pioneers can move toward decision-production with full focus, cautiously gauging choices and knowing the most suitable game-plan.

5. Better Stress Management:

Care supports pressure decrease, making a more quiet mental state for navigation. Pioneers who can oversee pressure are less inclined to settle on responsive choices and can keep calm even in testing circumstances.

6. Empathetic Understanding:

Care urges pioneers to tune in and feel for others effectively. This compassionate comprehension of colleagues' points of view improves the dynamic cycle by integrating different perspectives.

7. Improved Critical thinking Skills:

Careful pioneers succeed in critical thinking. By moving toward difficulties with a quiet and centered mind, they can separate complex issues, investigate inventive arrangements, and settle on choices that address underlying drivers instead of superficial side effects.

8. Enhanced Intuition:

Care develops an increased feeling of instinct. Pioneers can take advantage of their senses and premonitions, supplementing insightful reasoning with a more profound comprehension that goes past information and measurements.

9. Strategic Long haul Thinking:

Careful independent direction expands the time skyline of pioneers. They are bound to think about the drawn out ramifications of their decisions, adjusting choices to the all-encompassing objectives and vision of the association.

10. Promotion Of Comprehensive Choice Making:

Care cultivates a comprehensive way to deal with dynamic by empowering pioneers to think about different points of view. This inclusivity fortifies cooperation as well as prompts choices that mirror a more extensive comprehension of the hierarchical scene.

In outline, a careful methodology upgrades decision-production for pioneers by expanding mindfulness, controlling feelings, lessening predispositions, improving concentration, overseeing pressure, encouraging sympathetic comprehension, further developing critical thinking abilities, refining instinct, and advancing comprehensive navigation. These components by and large add to a more successful and insightful initiative style.

Chapter Five

"Driving With Sympathy: Building More Grounded Associations In The Work Environment"

Driving with sympathy is a groundbreaking methodology that rises above customary initiative ideal models, underscoring figuring out, empathy, and real association inside the work environment. At its center, sympathetic initiative includes the capacity to perceive, share, and answer the feelings of colleagues, cultivating a comprehensive and steady climate.

Sympathy constructs more grounded associations by recognizing the interesting encounters and points of view of every person. Pioneers who develop sympathy find opportunity to effectively tune in, approve feelings, and exhibit a veritable interest in the prosperity of their group. This makes a feeling of having a place and trust, establishing the groundwork for vigorous relational connections.

In the work environment, sympathetic pioneers not just consider the expert difficulties their group faces yet in addition perceive the individual perspectives that might affect execution. This all encompassing comprehension empowers pioneers to tailor support, give significant input, and address worries with a human-driven approach.

Compassion improves correspondence by advancing straightforwardness and transparency. Pioneers who lead with compassion encourage a climate where colleagues feel open to offering their viewpoints and concerns. This works with more compelling coordinated effort, as people are bound to contribute their one of a kind experiences when they feel esteemed and comprehended.

Besides, driving with sympathy adds to a positive hierarchical culture. It imparts a feeling of common perspective, energizes collaboration, and develops a strong climate where people are enabled to carry their valid selves to the work environment. At last, by driving with compassion, pioneers assemble more grounded relational associations as well as versatile and drawn in groups that add to generally work environment achievement.

Key Idea; The job of sympathy in developing positive administration and encouraging group associations.

The Job Of Sympathy In Developing Positive Leadership:

Sympathy assumes a vital part in developing positive initiative by encouraging a more profound comprehension of colleagues' feelings, encounters, and points of view. Pioneers who effectively practice sympathy make a working environment culture that focuses on empathy, trust, and open correspondence.

1. Understanding Group Dynamics:
Compassionate pioneers find opportunity to figure out the elements inside their groups. By perceiving individual qualities, difficulties, and inspirations, they can tailor administration methodologies to boost group adequacy.

2. Building Trust and Rapport:

Sympathy fabricates trust by showing a certified worry for the prosperity of colleagues. At the point when pioneers show that they comprehend and think often about the individual and expert parts of their group, it reinforces the obligations of trust and affinity.

3. Effective Communication:

Compassion upgrades correspondence by making a space for open exchange. Pioneers who feel for their colleagues can impart all the more successfully, guaranteeing that messages are gotten with understanding and thought for assorted points of view.

4. Conflict Resolution:

In the midst of contention, sympathetic pioneers approach circumstances with responsiveness. By recognizing and approving feelings, they work with a helpful goal process, transforming clashes into open doors for development and further developed group elements.

5. Motivating And Rousing Teams:

Compassionate pioneers move and persuade groups by interfacing on an individual level. Understanding the goals and provokes of colleagues permits pioneers to offer significant help and support, encouraging a positive and inspiring workplace.

The Job Of Compassion In Encouraging Group Connections:

Compassion fills in as an impetus for building more grounded group associations by establishing a climate where people feel seen, heard, and esteemed. This, thusly, adds to a cooperative and strong group dynamic.

1. Cultivating A Feeling Of Belonging:

Sympathetic pioneers encourage a feeling of having a place inside the group. By recognizing the uniqueness of each colleague and making a comprehensive climate, people feel esteemed for who they are, reinforcing their association with the group.

2. Encouraging Collaboration:

Group associations flourish with coordinated effort, and sympathy empowers a cooperative outlook. At the point when colleagues feel comprehended and upheld, they are bound to share thoughts, team up on projects, and add to aggregate achievement.

3. Boosting Confidence And Engagement:

Compassion emphatically impacts camaraderie and commitment. Pioneers who perceive and answer the feelings of their group make a more good and charming workplace, lifting the general mood and empowering dynamic interest.

4. Creating A Strong Culture:

Compassionate pioneers add to a strong group culture. By being sensitive to the requirements of people, pioneers can offer the important help, making a culture where colleagues feel open to looking for help and direction.

5. Enhancing Group Resilience:

Group associations are sustained through compassion, especially during testing times. Pioneers who relate to the battles of their group impart a feeling of shared strength, empowering the group to explore challenges along with an aggregate and strong soul.

In outline, sympathy is an essential component in certain initiative, encouraging group associations through grasping, trust, compelling correspondence, compromise, inspiration, and a feeling of having a place. By integrating compassion into initiative practices, pioneers add to a working environment culture that valucs individual commitments as well as reinforces the bonds that drive group achievement.

<u>Chapter Six</u>

"Developing A Development Outlook: An Initiative Objective"

Developing a development outlook remains as an administration basic, addressing a central change in how pioneers approach difficulties, learning, and improvement inside themselves and their groups. At its quintessence, a development outlook, instituted by clinician Ditty Dweck, is the conviction that capacities and insight can be created through commitment, difficult work, and tirelessness.

Pioneers who embrace a development outlook view disappointments not as long-lasting mishaps but rather as any open doors for learning and improvement. They comprehend that difficulties are innate chasing greatness and urge their groups to view misfortunes as venturing stones toward dominance.

This initiative basic includes encouraging a culture of consistent learning. Pioneers effectively search out potential open doors for individual and expert turn of events, demonstrating a promise to development that moves their groups. By showing a readiness to learn and adjust, pioneers establish a climate where colleagues feel urged to do likewise.

Besides, a development mentality advances advancement and strength. Pioneers who have confidence in the potential for development are bound to go ahead with reasonable courses of action, investigate groundbreaking thoughts, and explore vulnerabilities with an uplifting perspective. This drives hierarchical development as well as ingrains a feeling of versatility inside the group.

Key Idea; Techniques for creating and keeping a development situated outlook as a pioneer.

1. Embrace Difficulties As Opportunities:
View difficulties as opportunities for development, not unrealistic snags. Urge your group to handle

troublesome errands, underscoring the potential for learning and improvement.

2. Learn From Failures:

Shift the viewpoint on disappointments from misfortunes to venturing stones. Examine disappointments, separate significant illustrations, and use them as an establishment for future achievement. Share your own encounters of beating mishaps to rouse versatility.

3. Promote Persistent Learning:

Focus on continuous training and ability advancement. Go to studios, classes, or seek after additional instruction applicable to your influential position. Empower a culture of consistent advancing inside your group by giving assets and open doors to expertise improvement.

4. Seek Input And Valuable Criticism:

Embrace criticism as a method for development. Effectively look for input from your group and companions, esteeming assorted viewpoints. Utilize productive analysis to refine your authority approach and exhibit the significance of criticism to your group.

5. Set Stretch Goals:

Lay out aggressive yet attainable objectives that push both you and your group past your usual ranges of familiarity. Stretch objectives cultivate a development mentality by empowering consistent improvement and development.

6. Cultivate Curiosity:

Cultivate an inquisitive mentality by empowering investigation and curiosity. Remain open to groundbreaking thoughts and various perspectives. Model a feeling of interest, getting clarification on pressing issues and showing a real interest in gaining from others.

7. Acknowledge Exertion And Persistence:

Support the significance of exertion and constancy over natural ability. Celebrate difficult work and commitment inside your group, underlining that ceaseless exertion prompts improvement and achievement.

8. Encourage Hazard Taking:

Establish a protected climate for reasonable plans of action. Urge your group to try different things with novel thoughts and approaches. Regardless of whether results are not true to form, the experience adds to learning and development.

9. Model Adaptability:

Show versatility despite change. Embrace new difficulties with an uplifting perspective, showing your group that adaptability and versatility are basic parts of a development situated mentality.

10. Promote A Development Culture:

Implant a development outlook into your group's way of life. Empower open correspondence, coordinated effort, and the sharing of information. Encourage an air where everybody feels enabled to contribute thoughts and seek after persistent improvement.

Chapter Seven

"Careful Administration In The Midst Of Progress: Exploring Change Effectively"

Careful initiative in the midst of progress is an essential methodology that underlines present-second mindfulness, flexibility, and sympathetic decision-production to effectively explore changes. During times of progress, whether hierarchical rebuilding or market shifts, pioneers who embrace a careful methodology guide their groups through vulnerability with flexibility and lucidity.

At its center, careful initiative includes remaining sensitive to the ongoing conditions without being overpowered by previous encounters or future vulnerabilities. Pioneers develop a profound comprehension of the advancing scene, cultivating a feeling of quiet and concentration in the midst of the disturbance of progress.

Versatility is a sign of careful initiative during changes. Pioneers who practice care are more proficient at changing methodologies and embracing new points of view. This adaptability empowers them to answer insightfully to arising difficulties, guaranteeing a smoother progress for their groups.

Compassionate independent direction is another key component. Careful pioneers think about the close to home effect of progress in their groups and partners. By effectively tuning in, recognizing concerns, and showing getting it, they establish a climate where people feel upheld, cultivating an uplifting perspective even despite vulnerability.

Moreover, careful initiative advances powerful correspondence. Pioneers convey straightforwardly, keeping their groups informed about the changes, purposes for them, and the imagined results. This open correspondence fabricates trust and empowers a cooperative environment during the change.

Key Idea; Addressing how care adds to compelling initiative during times of progress.

Care fundamentally adds to successful initiative during times of progress by encouraging a grounded and versatile methodology that engages pioneers to explore vulnerability with strength and lucidity.

1. Present-Second Awareness:

Care develops present-second mindfulness, permitting pioneers to zero in on the ongoing circumstance without being excessively impacted by previous encounters or future nerves. This elevated mindfulness empowers pioneers to go with choices in view of the quick setting of the change, advancing smart and opportune activities.

2. Emotional Regulation:

During times of progress, feelings can run high among colleagues. Care outfits pioneers with the capacity to control their own feelings, forestalling receptive navigation. By keeping up with close to home equilibrium, pioneers can direct their groups with self-control, ingraining certainty and strength.

3. Adaptability And Flexibility:

Care cultivates flexibility, a pivotal quality in exploring change effectively. Pioneers with a careful methodology are more open to new viewpoints, adaptable in changing systems, and strong notwithstanding unforeseen difficulties. This flexibility guarantees that pioneers can direct their groups through the powerful scene of progress with a consistent and formed disposition.

4. Enhanced Choice Making:

Care adds to powerful direction by advancing clearness and concentration. Pioneers who practice care can slice through the commotion of vulnerability, focus on key goals, and pursue very much educated choices. This essential navigation is fundamental for guiding the association through advances with reason and course.

5. Empathetic Leadership:

Care upgrades sympathy, permitting pioneers to comprehend and address the worries and feelings of their colleagues during times of progress. By effectively tuning in, recognizing the difficulties, and exhibiting understanding, careful pioneers establish a steady climate that encourages trust and commitment.

6. Reduced Stress And Burnout:

The act of care diminishes pressure and burnout, normal difficulties during seasons of progress. Pioneers who focus on their own prosperity through care are better prepared to deal with the tensions of authority, guaranteeing supported viability all through the extraordinary interaction.

7. Effective Communication:

Care adds to clear and compelling correspondence. Pioneers can verbalize the vision behind the change, make sense of the reasoning, and keep their groups informed. Straightforward correspondence cultivates trust and arrangement, establishing a durable climate where everybody grasps their part in the change.

All in all, care is a foundation of powerful authority during times of progress. By advancing present-second mindfulness, profound guideline, versatility, improved navigation, compassionate initiative, and stress decrease, care outfits pioneers with the instruments to direct their groups through changes effectively, encouraging a positive and strong hierarchical culture.

Chapter Eight

"Rousing Development: A Positive Initiative Methodology"

Motivating development through a positive initiative methodology is tied in with making a working environment culture that cultivates imagination, cooperation, and a mentality equipped towards investigation and improvement. Good pioneers develop a climate where colleagues feel enabled to think past traditional limits and contribute inventive arrangements.

Fundamental to this approach is the support of chance taking. Positive pioneers perceive that development frequently includes venturing into a strange area and make a place of refuge where people can face challenges unafraid of pessimistic repercussions. This encourages a feeling of trial and error and receptiveness to groundbreaking thoughts.

Cultivating a development outlook is another key component. Positive pioneers ingrain the conviction that difficulties are open doors for learning and development. By stressing the benefit of gaining from disappointments and difficulties, pioneers make a culture that sees snags as venturing stones toward progress instead of unfavorable obstructions.

Straightforward correspondence is fundamental to moving development. Positive pioneers lay out channels that work with the open sharing of thoughts and criticism. Effectively standing by listening to different points of view, positive pioneers make discussions where creative thoughts can surface and be cooperatively investigated.

Acknowledgment and festivity assume a crucial part. Positive pioneers recognize both individual and group victories, supporting a culture that qualities and values inventive endeavors. This acknowledgment approves imaginative commitments as well as spurs people to keep pushing the limits of what is conceivable.

At last, through a positive administration approach, development becomes imbued in the hierarchical ethos, driving constant improvement, flexibility, and supported achievement.

Key Idea; How a positive outlook can fuel development and innovative reasoning inside groups.

A positive mentality fills in as a strong impetus for powering development and imaginative reasoning inside groups. At the point when colleagues take on an uplifting perspective, it establishes a favorable climate that supports interest, joint effort, and a readiness to investigate eccentric thoughts. This is the way a positive outlook pushes development:

1. Optimism Energizes Resilience:

A positive mentality ingrains confidence, empowering groups to move toward difficulties as any open doors instead of obstructions. When confronted with difficulties, colleagues with an uplifting perspective are stronger, returning rapidly and keeping up with excitement for tracking down imaginative arrangements.

2. Embracing A Development Mindset:

Energy lines up with a development outlook — a fundamental part of advancement. Colleagues who have confidence in their capacity to foster abilities and defeat difficulties are bound to embrace trial and error, gaining from disappointments, and ceaselessly looking for development.

3. Encouraging Chance Taking:

A positive outlook makes a culture that empowers determined risk-taking. Colleagues get a handle on more happy with venturing of their usual ranges of familiarity, proposing groundbreaking thoughts, and investigating imaginative methodologies when they accept their commitments are esteemed and upheld.

4. Fostering Cooperative Creativity:

Inspiration upgrades joint effort by cultivating a strong and liberal air. At the point when colleagues have an uplifting perspective on their cooperations, they are bound to share and expand upon one another's thoughts, prompting a synergistic inventive flow.

5. Boosting Inspiration And Engagement:

A positive mentality supports inspiration and commitment inside groups. At the point when people are roused, they are bound to put investment into investigating intelligent fixes. Positive pioneers assume a pivotal part in keeping up with camaraderie and inspiration.

6. Enhancing Critical Thinking Skills:

Energy improves critical thinking abilities by advancing a valuable and hopeful way to deal with difficulties. Colleagues with a positive mentality are better furnished to move toward issues with inventiveness, strength, and an emphasis on tracking down imaginative arrangements.

7. Cultivating A Culture Of Appreciation:

Energy includes perceiving and valuing the endeavors of colleagues. At the point when people feel esteemed, it makes a good criticism circle, empowering them to offer all the more effectively to the inventive flow and encouraging a culture where creative thoughts are recognized and celebrated.

8. Creating An Advancement Mindset:

A positive mentality makes way for a general development outlook inside the group. It moves the group's viewpoint from review imperatives as constraints to seeing opportunities for clever fixes. This mentality shift is fundamental for encouraging a ceaseless culture of development.

<u>Chapter Nine</u>

"Building A Positive Hierarchical Culture: Position Of Authority's"

Building a positive hierarchical culture is an intricate undertaking that pivots fundamentally on powerful initiative. Pioneers assume a urgent part in forming the qualities, standards, and in general environment inside a working environment. They act as the draftsmen of the hierarchical culture, impacting worker conduct and cultivating a feeling of solidarity.

Position of authority's in developing a positive culture includes setting a reasonable vision for the association. At the point when pioneers impart a convincing vision, workers gain a feeling of direction, cultivating commitment and responsibility. Besides, pioneers should epitomize the qualities they wish to ingrain, filling in as good examples for the ideal social credits.

Successful correspondence is one more basic part of administration in molding society. Pioneers ought to advance open and straightforward correspondence, establishing a climate where thoughts and input can stream unreservedly. This assists work with trusting and cooperation among colleagues.

Acknowledgment and appreciation are amazing assets in making a positive culture. Pioneers ought to recognize and compensate workers for their commitments, building up wanted ways of behaving and making a positive input circle. Moreover, advancing a solid balance between fun and serious activities and focusing on worker prosperity shows a guarantee to a positive culture.

Eventually, administration's impact on hierarchical culture is significant. Through vision-setting, correspondence, acknowledgment, and inclusivity, pioneers shape the establishment for a positive work environment culture that rouses representative commitment and hierarchical achievement.

Key Idea; Direction on molding a hierarchical culture that lines up with positive administration standards.

1. Define A Reasonable Vision:

Obviously articulate the association's central goal and values. Guarantee that these standards line up with positive initiative, underlining cooperation, regard, and a common feeling of direction.

2. Lead By Example:

Exhibit the ideal ways of behaving and esteems reliably. Pioneers act as good examples, and their activities essentially influence the authoritative culture. Model the energy and inclusivity you wish to find in the work environment.

3. Effective Communication:

Encourage open and straightforward correspondence channels. Keep workers informed about hierarchical objectives, changes, and triumphs. Energize input and make a culture where everybody feels happy with offering their viewpoints.

4. Recognition And Appreciation:

Execute acknowledgment programs that feature

representatives' commitments. Recognize and value the endeavors of people and groups routinely. Uplifting feedback supports wanted ways of behaving and encourages everyone.

5. Prioritize Representative Well-Being:

Show certifiable worry for the prosperity of your group. Advance balance between serious and fun activities, emotional wellness support, and establish a positive actual workplace. A sound labor force is bound to contribute emphatically to the hierarchical culture.

6. Encourage Collaboration:

Encourage a cooperative climate where cooperation is esteemed. Separate storehouses and advance cross-practical joint effort. Positive initiative includes making a feeling of solidarity and aggregate accomplishment.

7. Diversity And Inclusion:

Effectively advance variety and consideration drives. Guarantee that your administration group reflects variety and establish a comprehensive climate where all representatives feel appreciated and regarded.

8. Adaptability And Learning Culture:
Embrace change and energize a culture of constant learning. Positive pioneers consider difficulties to be potential open doors for development and cultivate an outlook that values transformation and development.

9. Feedback Mechanisms:
Lay out helpful input systems. Consistently request input from representatives and use it to settle on informed choices. This engages workers as well as adds to a culture of progress.

10. Empowerment And Trust: Agent obligations and engage representatives to simply decide. Trust is a foundation of good initiative, and when representatives feel trusted, they are bound to contribute emphatically to the hierarchical culture.

Chapter Ten

"Careful Administration In Virtual Groups: Exploring Remote Difficulties"

Careful authority in virtual groups is vital for exploring the special difficulties presented by remote work. Pioneers should develop a consciousness of their colleagues' prosperity and keep a careful way to deal with encourage a positive virtual workplace.

Without a trace of actual presence, viable correspondence becomes fundamental. Careful pioneers focus on clear and open correspondence, using different virtual instruments to connect holes and guarantee that colleagues feel associated. This incorporates customary registrations, virtual gatherings, and making stages for casual connections to construct brotherhood.

Understanding the assorted necessities of remote colleagues is one more key part of careful authority.

Recognizing the difficulties related with working from various areas and time regions, pioneers can tailor ways to deal with oblige individual inclinations and conditions. Adaptability turns into a foundation of careful initiative in virtual groups.

Building trust in a virtual setting depends vigorously on predictable and straightforward authority. Careful pioneers lay out assumptions obviously, commend accomplishments, and address concerns immediately. By cultivating a culture of trust, pioneers make an establishment for cooperation and development inside virtual groups.

Besides, careful initiative includes advancing balance between fun and serious activities in a distant setting. Empowering breaks, regarding non-working hours, and supporting representatives' general prosperity add to a positive virtual work culture.

Generally, careful initiative in virtual groups requires an uplifted consciousness of correspondence elements, individual necessities, and the significance of trust and balance between serious and fun activities. By exploring these difficulties with care, pioneers can really guide remote groups towards progress and establish a steady virtual workplace.

Key Idea; Adjusting positive initiative systems to actually lead remote groups.

Here are key contemplations to cultivate a positive and useful virtual workplace:

1. Clear Correspondence Channels: Underline straightforward correspondence. Obviously lucid assumptions, give normal updates, and lay out open channels for colleagues to put themselves out there. Positive pioneers keep the lines of correspondence open, diminishing vulnerability in a remote setting.

2. Virtual Group Building:
Set out open doors for virtual group building exercises. These can incorporate virtual get-togethers, cooperative activities, or casual video registrations. Positive pioneers grasp the significance of group union and effectively work to

fortify relational associations even in a remote setting.

3. Recognition And Appreciation: Carry out virtual acknowledgment projects to recognize individual and group accomplishments. Good pioneers guarantee that remote colleagues feel esteemed and appreciated for their commitments, cultivating a feeling of achievement and inspiration.

4. Flexibility And Empathy:
Recognize the interesting difficulties remote work models have for people. Positive pioneers display sympathy and adaptability, understanding that colleagues might have shifting conditions. Offering adaptable timetables and offering help where required shows a pledge to the prosperity of the remote group.

5. Goal Laying Out And Clarity: Obviously characterize objectives and assumptions. Positive pioneers set reachable targets, separate complex undertakings, and guarantee that remote colleagues grasp their jobs. Clearness in goals encourages a feeling of direction and heading, improving inspiration.

6. Encourage Autonomy:

Engage remote colleagues to take responsibility for work. Positive pioneers trust their groups, considering independence in direction. This advances a feeling of obligation and freedom, prompting expanded work fulfillment.

7. Continuous Learning And Development:

Encourage a culture of consistent learning. Positive pioneers put resources into the expert advancement of remote colleagues, giving open doors to ability upgrade and development. This advantages people as well as adds to the general outcome of the virtual group.

8. Technology And Tools:

Guarantee that remote groups approach the right innovation and instruments. Positive pioneers work with a consistent virtual work insight by putting resources into joint effort stages, project the board instruments, and preparing to improve computerized proficiency.

9. Regular Registrations And Feedback:

Timetable ordinary one-in one and group registrations. Positive pioneers give helpful criticism and effectively pay attention to the worries and thoughts of remote colleagues. Customary correspondence helps assemble trust and guarantees that everybody feels associated.

<u>Chapter Eleven</u>

"Making Comprehensive Administration: Cultivating Variety And Having A place"

Making comprehensive initiative includes encouraging a work environment culture that embraces variety and advances a feeling of having a place among all representatives. Comprehensive pioneers perceive and esteem individual contrasts, establishing a climate where everybody feels regarded, heard, and enabled.

Fundamental to comprehensive authority is the advancement of variety. Pioneers effectively look to differentiate groups by considering elements like race, orientation, age, nationality, and foundation. By building different groups, pioneers influence various points of view, abilities, and encounters, cultivating development and inventiveness inside the association.

Additionally, comprehensive pioneers go past simple portrayal, guaranteeing that different voices are heard and considered in dynamic cycles. They effectively look for input from people with various foundations and viewpoints, making a culture of inclusivity that qualities and coordinates different perspectives.

Cultivating a feeling of having a place is similarly critical. Comprehensive pioneers establish a climate where each representative feels invited and esteemed for what their identity is. This includes advancing inclusivity in authoritative strategies, practices, and correspondence, effectively tending to any predispositions that might exist.

Viable correspondence assumes a significant part in comprehensive administration. Pioneers ought to be straightforward and open, effectively sharing data about the association's obligation to variety and consideration. Clear correspondence assists work with trusting among representatives and supports the association's devotion to making a comprehensive working environment.

Preparing and instruction are key parts of making comprehensive authority. Pioneers ought to put resources into programs that improve familiarity with oblivious predispositions, social ability, and comprehensive practices. This guarantees that pioneers are furnished with the information and abilities to cultivate a comprehensive climate.

Eventually, making a comprehensive initiative includes a ceaseless obligation to cultivating variety, value, and having a place. By embracing and praising contrasts, esteeming different viewpoints, and effectively attempting to dispense with predispositions, pioneers add to a work environment culture where everybody feels included, upheld, and engaged to flourish.

Key Idea; The connection between certain initiatives and making a comprehensive working environment.

The connection between sure initiative and making a comprehensive working environment is fundamental to encouraging a culture that values variety and guarantees a feeling of having a place for all representatives. Positive pioneers effectively add to a comprehensive climate through a few key components:

1. Embracing Diversity:

Positive pioneers comprehend the strength that variety brings to the work environment. They effectively try to fabricate different groups, perceiving that a scope of points of view, foundations, and encounters improves innovativeness and critical thinking. By embracing variety, positive pioneers set the establishment for a comprehensive working environment.

2. Esteeming Individual Differences:

Comprehensive pioneers appreciate and esteem the uniqueness of each colleague. They perceive that distinctions in viewpoints, abilities, and qualities add to the general progress of the association. This appreciation makes an environment where representatives feel saw the truth about and regarded.

3. Open Communication:

Positive pioneers encourage open and straightforward correspondence. They establish a climate where workers feel happy with communicating their thoughts and concerns. This transparency adds to a culture of inclusivity, guaranteeing that different voices are heard and considered in dynamic cycles.

4. Laying Out Comprehensive Policies:

Authority assumes a significant part in molding hierarchical strategies. Positive pioneers effectively work to make and support approaches that advance inclusivity. This incorporates fair recruiting rehearses, equivalent open doors for professional success, and a guarantee to killing predispositions in all parts of the working environment.

5. Offering Help And Recognition:

Comprehensive pioneers offer help to all workers, recognizing their commitments and giving open doors to development. Acknowledgment programs that celebrate different accomplishments support a positive and comprehensive work environment culture. This help makes a feeling of having a place and urges people to carry their valid selves to work.

6. Demonstrating Comprehensive Behavior:

Positive pioneers show others how its done. They model comprehensive way of behaving by approaching everybody with deference, showing sympathy, and effectively exhibiting a pledge to variety. By typifying these qualities, pioneers motivate others to embrace inclusivity in their cooperations and coordinated efforts.

7. Ceaseless Learning And Adaptation:

Comprehensive initiative includes a guarantee to persistent learning. Positive pioneers stay informed about variety and incorporation best practices, effectively looking for ways of improving and adjust their administration style. This continuous responsibility guarantees that the association advances pair with the changing scene of inclusivity.

Generally, positive initiative and inclusivity are interconnected components that add to a flourishing working environment culture. At the point when pioneers effectively embrace variety, impart transparently, lay out comprehensive strategies, offer help, model comprehensive way of behaving, and focus on consistent learning, they establish a climate where each representative feels esteemed, regarded, and included. This, thusly, prompts upgraded cooperation, development, and in general hierarchical achievement.

Chapter Twelve

"Careful Compromise: Exploring Conflicts With Energy"

Careful compromise is a methodology that includes exploring conflicts with a positive and smart mentality. It coordinates the standards of care - being available, mindful, and non-critical - to encourage productive correspondence and figuring out notwithstanding clashes.

Vital to careful compromise is the development of mindfulness. People took part in struggle evaluate their feelings, viewpoints, and responses, perceiving the expected predispositions or triggers that might heighten the conflict. By remaining present at the time, people can move toward the contention with a more clear comprehension of their own feelings and inspirations.

Positive language and deferential openness are absolutely vital parts of careful compromise. People express their interests or viewpoints utilizing valuable language, staying away from fault or analysis. Undivided attention becomes critical, with each party completely participated in figuring out the other's perspective. This advances compassion and establishes a favorable climate for settling on some shared interest.

Careful compromise additionally includes zeroing in on arrangements as opposed to harping on the issue. By mutually investigating choices and split the difference, people work cooperatively to arrive at goals that address the fundamental issues. This approach encourages a positive, arrangement situated outlook that adds to long haul relationship building.

In addition, consolidating care practices, for example, profound breathing or brief snapshots of reflection during the contention can assist with overseeing pressure and forestall acceleration. By moving toward clashes with a careful demeanor, people add to a positive and conscious hierarchical culture that values open correspondence and productive critical thinking.

Key Idea; Methods for settling clashes with a positive initiative outlook.

1. Active Listening:

Practice undivided attention by focusing completely on the individual communicating their interests. Guarantee you comprehend their point of view prior to answering. This exhibits regard and cultivates open correspondence.

2. Empathy Building:

Develop compassion by imagining the other individual's perspective. Comprehend their sentiments and inspirations, recognizing that alternate points of view add to a more extravagant comprehension of the circumstance.

3. Use Positive Language:

Outline your reactions with positive language. Rather than zeroing in on fault or analysis, offer your viewpoints in a way that underlines cooperation and tracking down arrangements. This keeps a productive tone.

4. Focus On Solutions:

Empower an answer situated mentality. Instead of harping on the issue, work cooperatively to distinguish likely arrangements. This approach moves the concentration from fault to figuring out something worth agreeing on.

5. Clarify Expectations:

Obviously well-spoken assumptions and guarantee that the two players have a mutual perspective of jobs and obligations. Mistaken assumptions frequently add to clashes, and clearness can forestall future conflicts.

6. Seek Normal Ground:

Distinguish areas of arrangement and expand on them. Settling on some shared interest lays out an establishment for settling clashes and advances a feeling of solidarity among colleagues.

7. Mindful Communication:

Coordinate care rehearses into your correspondence. Take short delays to gather your contemplations, and urge others to do likewise. Careful correspondence cultivates a quiet and smart climate during compromise.

8. Encourage Valuable Feedback:

Establish a climate where valuable criticism is invited. Lay out a culture that values criticism as a device for development, permitting colleagues to communicate worries unafraid of backlash.

9. Mediation And Facilitation:

If vital, include an impartial outsider to intercede or work with the goal interaction. This can give a fair viewpoint and guide the discussion toward a positive result.

10. Follow-Up And Reflection:

After a contention is settled, circle back to the elaborate gatherings to guarantee that the arrangements are executed and that the functioning relationship gets to the next level. Consider the compromise interaction to distinguish regions for persistent improvement.

By integrating these methods into compromise processes, pioneers can move toward conflicts with a positive outlook, encouraging a culture of open correspondence, joint effort, and constant improvement inside the group or association.

Chapter Thirteen

"Initiative Presence: Making A Positive Picture In The Business World"

Initiative presence includes the specialty of making a positive and compelling picture in the business world. It goes past simple power and envelops the capacity to motivate, draw in, and convey certainty. Building initiative presence is pivotal for viable correspondence, navigation, and generally speaking effect inside an association.

One part of administration presence is keeping up with validness. Pioneers who genuinely express their qualities and convictions fabricate trust and believability. Validness impacts others and lays out a certifiable association, encouraging a positive picture.

Certainty is a foundation of initiative presence. Pioneers ooze certainty through their non-verbal communication, manner of speaking, and definitiveness. A certain pioneer motivates trust and consoles partners, making a positive view of their capacity to explore difficulties.

Viable correspondence is vital in forming administration presence. Pioneers articulate their vision and thoughts with clearness, effectively pay attention to other people, and adjust their correspondence style to different crowds. Positive correspondence encourages understanding and advances a great picture.

Developing capacity to understand people on a deeper level contributes fundamentally to initiative presence. Pioneers who get it and deal with their feelings, as well as those of others, exhibit compassion and appeal. This capacity to understand individuals on a deeper level aides construct positive connections and reinforces the general presence of a pioneer.

Initiative presence stretches out past individual connections to envelop a more extensive effect on hierarchical culture. Pioneers who encourage a positive and comprehensive working environment add to a great picture both inside and remotely. By focusing on values, credibility, certainty, powerful correspondence, and the capacity to understand people on a deeper level, pioneers can create a convincing and positive presence that resounds in the business world.

Key Idea; Upgrading initiative presence through a positive and careful methodology.

Improving initiative presence through a positive and careful methodology includes developing mindfulness, encouraging credible associations, and making a positive effect on the hierarchical culture. This is an aide en route to accomplish this:

1. Self-Reflection And Awareness:

Participate in ordinary self-reflection to figure out your qualities, assets, and regions for development. Careful pioneers know about their feelings and responses, permitting them to answer nicely to circumstances. This mindfulness frames the establishment for a positive initiative presence.

2. Authenticity In Communication:

Speak with validness, adjusting your words and activities to your qualities. Be veritable and straightforward, as genuineness fabricates trust. Careful pioneers talk with clearness, staying away from language, and putting themselves out there in a way that reverberates with different crowds.

3. Active Listening:

Practice undivided attention to grasp the viewpoints and worries of others. Careful pioneers really focus, keeping away from interferences, and exhibit sympathy. This encourages significant associations and adds to a positive initiative presence.

4. Positive Body Language:

Be aware of your non-verbal communication, as it assumes an essential part in initiative presence. Keep up with open and congenial signals, visually connect, and utilize non-verbal prompts that convey certainty and energy.

5. Encourage Inclusivity:

Encourage a comprehensive climate where various voices are esteemed. Careful pioneers effectively look for input from all colleagues, advancing a feeling of having a place. Inclusivity adds to a positive hierarchical culture and upgrades initiative presence.

6. Mindful Choice Making:

Move toward decision-production with care, taking into account the drawn out influence on people and the association. Careful pioneers weigh choices, look for assorted viewpoints, and settle on choices that line up with their qualities and the prosperity of the group.

7. Gratitude And Recognition:

Offer thanks and acknowledgment for the commitments of others. Careful pioneers recognize accomplishments and show appreciation, making a positive climate that spurs and moves the group.

8. Continuous Learning And Adaptation:

Embrace a mentality of persistent learning. Remain open to groundbreaking thoughts, input, and potential open doors for development. Careful pioneers adjust to changes with strength, adding to a positive initiative presence that oozes certainty and adaptability.

9. Promote Work-Life Balance:

Support a solid balance between serious and fun activities among colleagues. Careful pioneers perceive the significance of prosperity and urge rehearses that add to a positive and reasonable workplace.

10. Cultivate A Positive Hierarchical Culture:

Encourage a positive hierarchical culture by advancing qualities like cooperation, development, and regard. A careful way to deal with initiative adds to a climate where people flourish, improving generally initiative presence.

By coordinating these careful practices into initiative, people can upgrade their presence, decidedly influence the working environment, and encourage a culture of legitimacy, compassion, and persistent improvement.

Chapter Fourteen

"Versatile Initiative: Exploring Vulnerability With A Positive Mentality"

Versatile initiative is a powerful methodology that includes exploring vulnerability with a positive mentality, adaptability, and flexibility. In a consistently evolving scene, versatile pioneers flourish by embracing difficulties and encouraging a culture of nonstop learning and development.

Integral to versatile initiative is a positive mentality that sees vulnerability not as a danger, but rather as a chance for development. Pioneers develop confidence, moving their groups to embrace change and view difficulties as venturing stones to progress. This mentality establishes the vibe for an association's way of life, advancing flexibility and a proactive reaction to vulnerability.

Adaptability is a center quality of versatile initiative. Pioneers should change procedures, cycles, and, surprisingly, long haul objectives in light of moving conditions. By exhibiting versatility, pioneers engage their groups to explore change with certainty and add to the association's general strength.

Successful correspondence is central in versatile authority. Pioneers keep their groups informed, giving clearness on hierarchical objectives and changes. Straightforward correspondence fabricates trust and guarantees that everybody is in total agreement, cultivating a feeling of aggregate liability during questionable times.

Integrating a constant learning mentality is one more key component of versatile initiative. Pioneers energize trial and error, celebrate the two victories and disappointments, and advance a culture that values progressing improvement. This approach improves individual and group abilities as well as adds to authoritative dexterity.

Versatility is the last mainstay of versatile authority. Pioneers motivate flexibility by recognizing mishaps, gaining from them, and pushing ahead sincerely. This good versatility encourages a culture where people feel upheld and persuaded to defeat difficulties, adding to supported progress despite vulnerability.

Key Idea; How pioneers can adjust emphatically to eccentric and unsure circumstances.

Pioneers can adjust emphatically to capricious and dubious circumstances by embracing adaptability, cultivating flexibility, keeping a positive outlook, and utilizing viable correspondence. Here is an aide on exploring vulnerability with a positive methodology:

1. Flexibility and Agility:

Support an adaptable mentality inside the initiative group. Be available to changing plans and methodologies in view of advancing conditions. Embrace change as a chance for development, and advance spryness in decision-production to answer rapidly to unexpected difficulties.

2. Resilience Building:

Foster strength as a center initiative quality. Recognize misfortunes, gain from them, and support a versatile disposition among colleagues. Strong pioneers return from difficulty, moving their groups to confront vulnerability with a positive and decided standpoint.

3. Positive Mindset:

Develop a positive outlook that considers difficulties to be potential open doors. Center around what can be controlled as opposed to harping on what can't. Pioneers who approach vulnerability with hopefulness rouse certainty and inspiration in their groups, cultivating a mental fortitude.

4. Effective Communication:

Keep up with straightforward and open correspondence channels. Keep the group informed about changes, challenges, and the general vision. Clear correspondence diminishes uneasiness and vulnerability among colleagues, encouraging trust and a feeling of aggregate reason.

5. Empowering Teams:

Enable groups to contribute arrangements and thoughts. In dubious circumstances, various points of view are important. Pioneers who include their groups in direction establish a cooperative climate that upgrades critical thinking and versatility.

6. Continuous Learning:

Advance a culture of consistent learning. Empower pioneers and colleagues to obtain new abilities, remain refreshed on industry drifts, and adjust to arising difficulties. A learning mentality upgrades versatility and prepares the group to explore vulnerabilities with capability.

7. Scenario Planning:

Direct situation arranging activities to plan for various possible results. This proactive methodology permits pioneers to expect difficulties and devise techniques for different situations, limiting the effect of unexpected occasions.

8. Crisis Preparedness:

Create and routinely update emergency the executives plans. Pioneers who are ready for potential emergencies can answer quickly and really, relieving the effect of questionable circumstances on the association.

<u>Chapter Fifteen</u>

"The Specialty Of Assignment: Positive Authority In Enabling Groups"

The specialty of designation is a key part of positive initiative, underlining trust, joint effort, and strengthening inside groups. Designating really is something beyond relegating undertakings; it includes cultivating a culture where colleagues feel esteemed and enabled to contribute their abilities and skill.

Positive pioneers perceive the qualities and abilities of their colleagues. By assigning undertakings that line up with individual qualities, pioneers engage their groups to succeed in their particular regions. This improves by and large group execution as well as develops a feeling of achievement and occupation fulfillment.

Trust is a foundation of effective designation. Positive pioneers trust their colleagues to independently take responsibility for undertakings and simply decide. This trust lifts group confidence level as well as empowers individual development and expert turn of events.

Openness is of the utmost importance in the craft of appointment. Pioneers ought to obviously convey assumptions, give fundamental assets, and proposition continuous help. By keeping up with open lines of correspondence, good pioneers guarantee that colleagues figure out their jobs and feel positive about their assigned liabilities.

Designating likewise advances a cooperative and comprehensive climate. Positive pioneers include colleagues in dynamic cycles, looking for their feedback and esteeming assorted points of view. This cooperative methodology advances the nature of results as well as reinforces the feeling of having a place and commitment inside the group.

Eventually, the specialty of designation in sure administration is tied in with making a culture of trust, strengthening, and cooperation. Pioneers who ace this craftsmanship develop high-performing groups that blossom with shared objectives and individual qualities.

Key Idea; Procedures for powerful designation that line up with positive administration standards.

1. Know Your Team:

Grasp the qualities, abilities, and inclinations of each colleague. Positive pioneers tailor their designation approach in light of individual capacities, guaranteeing undertakings line up with colleagues' aptitude and interests.

2. Clear Communication:

Impart assumptions plainly. Positive pioneers articulate the objectives, wanted results, and a particular directions related with designated undertakings. Clearness diminishes errors and enables colleagues to succeed.

3. Provide Satisfactory Resources:

Outfit your group with the essential assets, devices, and data to effectively finish appointed jobs. Positive pioneers guarantee that their group has everything expected to really achieve their obligations.

4. Encourage Questions And Feedback:

Encourage a climate where colleagues feel open to seeking clarification on some pressing issues and giving criticism. Positive pioneers invite input, guaranteeing that everybody is in total agreement and elevating a cooperative way to deal with designation.

5. Build Trust:

Trust is key to powerful assignment. Positive pioneers trust their colleagues to take responsibility for. This trust cultivates a feeling of obligation and independence, improving both individual and group execution.

6. Match Assignments To Skills:

Adjust assignments to the abilities and qualities of each colleague. Positive pioneers consider individual abilities while designating, amplifying the potential for progress and helping colleagues' certainty.

7. Provide Valuable Open Doors For Growth:

Delegate errands that proposition learning open doors. Positive pioneers view designation for the purpose of encouraging proficient turn of events. This approach energizes consistent acquiring and ability upgrade inside the group.

8. Set Sensible Expectations:

Lay out attainable objectives and cutoff times. Positive pioneers comprehend the significance of setting sensible assumptions to forestall overpower and guarantee a good outcome. Reasonable objectives add to a positive and persuaded group.

9. Acknowledge And Observe Success:

Perceive and celebrate accomplishments coming about because of designated errands. Positive pioneers express appreciation and recognize the commitments of colleagues, supporting a positive culture of acknowledgment and prize.

10. Maintain Open Lines Of Communication:

Keep correspondence channels open all through the assignment cycle. Positive pioneers energize progressing conversations, registrations, and updates. This guarantees that colleagues feel upheld and can look for direction if necessary.

11. Lead By Example:

Show a readiness to designate inside your influential position. Positive pioneers show others how its done, showing that designation is a cooperative and enabling practice. This establishes the vibe for a positive and powerful designation process.

By carrying out these procedures, positive pioneers can improve the viability of designation, cultivating a culture of joint effort, trust, and nonstop development inside their groups.

Chapter Sixteen

"Careful Using Time effectively: An Initiative Fundamental For Enduring Achievement"

Careful using time effectively is a significant initiative expertise that includes deliberate and cognizant distribution of time to errands and needs. Pioneers who practice careful time usage center around improving efficiency, diminishing pressure, and making enduring progress for them as well as their groups.

At its center, careful using time productively includes defining clear boundaries and objectives. Pioneers recognize undertakings that line up with hierarchical goals and distribute time in light of their importance. By deliberately picking where to contribute their time, chiefs guarantee that endeavors add to long haul achievement.

Careful pioneers likewise stress present-second mindfulness, staying away from performing multiple tasks and focusing completely on each assignment in turn. This approach improves concentration and nature of work, lessening blunders and cultivating a feeling of achievement.

Successful designation is one more part of careful using time effectively. Pioneers circulate undertakings in light of colleagues' assets and mastery, enhancing efficiency. Assigning enables colleagues, permitting pioneers to focus on high-influence liabilities.

Careful using time productively consolidates standard reflection and change. Pioneers survey the viability of their time designation, recognize regions for development, and make vital changes in accordance with upgrade effectiveness.

Also, careful using time productively incorporates key breaks and taking care of oneself. Pioneers perceive the significance of rest and revival to keep up with supported efficiency and forestall burnout.

By coordinating careful using time productively into their administration approach, pioneers establish a climate of effectiveness, concentration, and equilibrium. This prompts individual accomplishment as well as adds to the enduring achievement and prosperity of the whole group and association.

Key Idea; Time usage tips for pioneers to keep a positive outlook and achievement.

1. Prioritize Tasks:

Recognize and focus on errands in view of significance and cutoff times. Center around high-influence exercises that line up with hierarchical objectives. This guarantees that your time is put resources into exercises that contribute fundamentally to progress.

2. Set Clear Goals:

Lay out clear present moment and long haul objectives. Obviously characterized objectives give guidance and motivation, directing your time usage choices and cultivating a positive mentality based on accomplishment.

3. Effective Planning:

Plan your day, week, and month decisively. Use instruments like schedules and organizers to plan errands and distribute time effectively. Viable arranging limits last-minute pressure and considers a proactive way to deal with using time productively.

4. Learn To Delegate:

Perceive the qualities of your group and representative errands as needs be. Assigning enables colleagues and permits you to zero in on high-need liabilities. A positive mentality is developed when pioneers trust their group and team up successfully.

5. Practice Careful Focus:

Embrace careful spotlight by focusing on each undertaking in turn. Stay away from performing various tasks, as it can prompt diminished efficiency and expanded pressure. Careful center upgrades the nature of work and adds to a positive outlook.

6. Regular Breaks:

Plan standard breaks to forestall burnout and keep up with mental clearness. Brief breaks work on by and large efficiency, innovativeness, and prosperity.

Pioneers who focus on taking care of oneself keep a positive and stimulated mentality.

7. Adaptability:

Embrace versatility in your timetable. Unexpected conditions might emerge, and an adaptable methodology permits pioneers to explore difficulties with versatility. Keeping a positive outlook during startling changes is fundamental for progress.

8. Learn To Say No:

Perceive your cutoff points and figure out how to express no to undertakings that don't line up with your needs. Pioneers who put down stopping points focus on their prosperity and keep a positive outlook by zeroing in on the main thing.

9. Continuous Learning:

Commit time to continuous mastering and expertise improvement. Remaining refreshed on industry patterns and securing new information adds to individual and expert development. Consistent learning encourages a positive and ground breaking mentality.

10. Celebrate Achievements:

Recognize and celebrate achievements, both of all shapes and sizes. Considering victories ingrains a positive outlook and inspires pioneers to keep taking a stab at greatness. Perceiving accomplishments likewise lifts group feeling of confidence.

By integrating these time usage tips into their everyday practices, pioneers can keep a positive outlook, improve efficiency, and add to long haul accomplishment for them as well as their groups.

<u>**Chapter Seventeen**</u>

"Driving Through Emergency: A Positive Administration Outlook In Difficult Stretches"

Driving through an emergency requests a positive initiative outlook that motivates strength, cultivates solidarity, and guides associations through fierce times. Positive initiative during emergencies is described by flexibility, compassion, and a pledge to keeping up with spirit.

Taking on a positive outlook includes reexamining difficulties as any open doors for development and advancement. Pioneers who convey hopefulness and trust notwithstanding affliction rouse their groups to go up against difficulties with strength and inventiveness. This mentality fills in as an encouraging sign, directing the association toward helpful arrangements.

Compassion turns into a foundation of positive initiative during emergencies. Pioneers who get it and recognize the profound effect of vulnerability and change establish a steady climate. Paying attention to worries, showing getting it, and offering close to home help encourage trust and attachment among colleagues.

Straightforwardness is fundamental for positive initiative during emergencies. Conveying straightforwardly about the circumstance, difficulties, and potential arrangements assembles trust and mitigates uneasiness. Pioneers who share a reasonable and genuine evaluation of the conditions make a feeling of solidarity and reason.

Vital navigation is a critical part of positive initiative in testing times. Pioneers should go with difficult decisions while considering the prosperity of their groups. Straightforwardly conveying choices and making sense of their reasoning assists colleagues with understanding the way ahead, building up a positive and bound together front.

In addition, positive pioneers effectively look for open doors for learning and development during emergencies. By adjusting to new data and constantly reevaluating procedures, pioneers exhibit spryness and obligation to conquering difficulties.

Basically, driving through an emergency with a positive mentality includes developing versatility, sympathy, straightforwardness, and a promise to consistent improvement. Positive pioneers move certainty, encourage solidarity, and guide their associations toward long haul achievement even notwithstanding difficulty.

Key Idea; Experiences on keeping a positive initiative methodology during testing conditions.

Keeping a positive initiative methodology during testing conditions requires key experiences and purposeful activities. Here are key bits of knowledge to cultivate energy and guide pioneers through affliction:

1. Resilience As An Initiative Trait:

Comprehend that strength is an imperative initiative quality during testing times. Pioneers who show flexibility move certainty and confidence in their groups. Perceive mishaps as impermanent and view difficulties as any open doors for development.

2. Transparent Communication:

Embrace straightforward correspondence as a key part of positive initiative. Keep your group what is going on, challenges, and the association's reaction. Straightforward correspondence constructs trust, cultivating a feeling of shared liability and reason.

3. Empathetic Leadership:

Focus on compassion in administration. Grasp the profound effect of testing conditions in your colleagues. Recognize their interests, offer help, and effectively tune in. Compassionate pioneers establish a steady climate that supports confidence.

4. Focus On Solutions:

Shift the concentration from issues to arrangements. Positive pioneers approach difficulties with a critical thinking mentality. Urge your group to conceptualize clever fixes, underlining a proactive and ground breaking approach.

5. Adaptability And Flexibility:

Embrace flexibility as a center initiative guideline. Conditions might change quickly, and pioneers who adjust rapidly exhibit versatility and deftness. Be adaptable in changing methodologies and plans depending on the situation to explore vulnerabilities.

6. Team Collaboration:

Encourage a cooperative group climate. Empower open correspondence, thought sharing, and cooperation. A unified group pursuing shared objectives reinforces versatility and adds to a positive hierarchical culture.

7. Continuous Learning:

Embrace an outlook of nonstop learning. Pioneers who look for open doors for development, remain informed about industry drifts, and adjust to new data exhibit a promise to progress. Persistent learning adds to versatility and positive authority.

8. Recognize and Observe Little Wins:

Recognize and celebrate little triumphs en route. Perceiving accomplishments, regardless of how steady, lifts the general mood and builds up a positive mentality inside the group. Celebrating progress gives inspiration during testing times.

9. Lead By Example:

Show the uplifting outlook and ways of behaving you wish to find in your group. Pioneers who show others how its done established the vibe for the hierarchical culture. Showing positive thinking, versatility, and strength urges your group to stick to this same pattern.

10. Encourage Well-Being:

Focus on the prosperity of your colleagues. Empower breaks, support balance between fun and serious activities, and give assets to psychological wellness. Pioneers who effectively elevate prosperity add to a positive and supportable group dynamic.

By coordinating these bits of knowledge into their initiative methodology, pioneers can keep a positive outlook during testing conditions, move their groups, and explore vulnerabilities with versatility and effortlessness.

Chapter Eighteen

"Encouraging Worker Prosperity: A Positive Initiative Goal"

Encouraging worker prosperity has turned into a foundation of positive initiative, perceiving that the wellbeing and bliss of representatives are fundamental for hierarchical achievement. Positive pioneers comprehend that representative prosperity goes past customary advantages and includes an all encompassing methodology that supports physical, mental, and profound wellbeing.

A positive initiative basic for cultivating representative prosperity includes establishing a strong workplace. This incorporates advancing balance between serious and fun activities, giving assets to push the board, and offering adaptability to oblige individual requirements. By recognizing the significance of a decent way of life, pioneers add to a better and more propelled labor force.

Openness is of the utmost importance in this goal. Positive pioneers transparently talk about the meaning of prosperity, lessening the disgrace encompassing emotional well-being, and empowering open discourse. Straightforward correspondence guarantees that workers feel open to looking for help while required, adding to a culture of trust and compassion.

Acknowledgment and appreciation are indispensable parts. Positive pioneers effectively recognize and celebrate accomplishments, both of all shapes and sizes. Perceiving commitments cultivates a feeling of significant worth and achievement, adding to the general prosperity of representatives.

Besides, pioneers who put resources into proficient improvement potential open doors and expertise upgrade show a guarantee to the development and satisfaction of their representatives. This upgrades work fulfillment as well as advances a positive hierarchical culture based on persistent learning.

Generally, cultivating representative prosperity as a positive initiative basic includes making a work environment that focuses on all encompassing wellbeing, energizes open correspondence, perceives commitments, and gives valuable open doors to individual and expert development. This approach not just improves the general nature of work life yet additionally adds to authoritative achievement and representative maintenance.

Key Idea; The job of pioneers in advancing prosperity and energy among colleagues.

Pioneers assume a significant part in advancing prosperity and energy among colleagues by cultivating a strong and positive workplace. Here are key parts of the pioneer's job in improving the prosperity of their group:

1. Cultivate A Positive Culture:

Pioneers set the vibe for authoritative culture. By advancing energy, strength, and a useful outlook, pioneers develop a climate where colleagues feel esteemed, roused, and upheld.

2. Prioritize Work-Life Balance:

Support a solid balance between serious and fun activities by regarding limits and advancing sensible working hours. Pioneers who focus on balance add to diminished pressure, expanded work fulfillment, and worked on by and large prosperity among colleagues.

3. Open Communication:

Work with open and straightforward correspondence. Pioneers who effectively tune in, support criticism, and convey straightforwardly make a culture of trust. Colleagues feel happy with communicating concerns or looking for help, adding to a good work environment.

4. Recognition And Appreciation:

Perceive and value the commitments of colleagues. Customary affirmation of accomplishments, both individual and group, lifts everyone's spirits and builds up a positive feeling of achievement inside the group.

5. Provide Assets For Well-Being:

Offer assets and backing for prosperity drives. Pioneers can give admittance to emotional well-being assets, wellbeing projects, or stress the executives devices, exhibiting a guarantee to the all encompassing soundness of their group.

6. Set Clear Expectations:

Obviously convey assumptions and objectives. Distinct assumptions decrease equivocalness and enable colleagues to perform with certainty, encouraging a positive feeling of direction and achievement.

7. Encourage Proficient Development:

Put resources into the expert improvement of colleagues. Pioneers who give amazing open doors to expertise improvement and profession development add to the general prosperity and occupation fulfillment of their group.

8. Flexibility And Adaptability:

Embrace adaptability and versatility. Pioneers who are available to adaptable work plans and comprehend the different requirements of their group add to a positive and comprehensive workplace.

Chapter Nineteen

"Careful Systems administration: Building Positive Expert Connections"

Careful systems administration includes building positive expert associations with a cognizant and purposeful methodology. It goes past conventional systems administration techniques by underscoring genuine associations, undivided attention, and shared help. This careful way to deal with systems administration encourages significant connections that add to proficient development and achievement.

In careful systems administration, people approach communications with a certified interest in others. This includes undivided attention to figure out the necessities, objectives, and points of view of individual experts. By exhibiting sympathy and being completely present in discussions, people make an establishment for bona fide associations.

Positive and valuable correspondence is essential to careful systems administration. This incorporates communicating one's thoughts plainly, articulating objectives, and offering some benefit to other people. By developing a positive correspondence style, people add to a steady systems administration climate.

Correspondence assumes an essential part in careful systems administration. People look for chances to help others, whether through sharing information, giving presentations, or offering help. This common help reinforces connections and fabricates an organization established on joint effort and trust.

Careful systems administration likewise includes an essential way to deal with building and keeping up with connections. People distinguish people or gatherings lined up with their expert objectives, concentrate profoundly on developing associations, and support connections after some time. This purposeful methodology guarantees that the organization is both significant and pertinent.

Generally, careful systems administration is tied in with encouraging valid associations, rehearsing positive correspondence, embracing correspondence, and decisively assembling connections. By drawing nearer coordinating with care and purposefulness, experts can make a steady organization that adds to their own and proficient turn of events.

Key Idea; Utilizing positive authority standards for viable systems administration and relationship-building.

Utilizing positive initiative standards upgrades the viability of systems administration and relationship-building, making an establishment for significant associations and expert achievement. This is the way certain initiative standards can applied to organize:

1. Authenticity:

Positive pioneers focus on validness, bringing their actual selves into proficient connections. In systems administration, being valid encourages veritable associations. Share your encounters, values, and goals to fabricate connections established on truthfulness.

2. Empathy And Dynamic Listening:

Integrate sympathy and undivided attention into systems administration. Positive pioneers really care about others' points of view and effectively pay attention to grasp their requirements. By sympathizing with individual experts, you make associations in view of understanding and backing.

3. Positive Communication:

Apply positive correspondence standards to systems administration. Outline discussions in a hopeful and useful way. Energy in correspondence makes connections more charming as well as adds to a good impression.

4. Reciprocity:

Embrace the standard of correspondence in systems administration. Positive pioneers look for chances to offer some incentive to other people, whether through sharing bits of knowledge, offering help, or making presentations. This proportional mentality fortifies connections over the long haul.

5. Inclusivity:

Apply inclusivity in systems administration by esteeming different viewpoints and cultivating a comprehensive climate. Positive pioneers effectively look for associations with people from various foundations, ventures, and encounters, expanding the extent of their organization.

6. Gratitude:

Offer thanks in systems administration associations. Positive pioneers recognize and value the commitments of others, whether it's recommendation, mentorship, or cooperation. Appreciation constructs a positive climate and fortifies proficient bonds.

7. Strategic Relationship-Building:

Relationship-building directed by certain initiative standards. Recognize people or gatherings lined up with your qualities and expert objectives. Focus intensely on developing significant associations and support connections after some time.

8. Continuous Learning And Growth:

Embrace a mentality of constant learning and development in systems administration. Positive pioneers effectively look for chances to extend their insight, abilities, and associations. This obligation to development upgrades the profundity and pertinence of expert connections.

9. Adaptability:

Apply flexibility to explore different systems administration circumstances. Positive pioneers are adaptable in their methodology, adjusting to various characters and conditions. This versatility cultivates a positive and comprehensive systems administration experience.

10. Leadership by Example:

Exhibit positive administration through your activities in systems administration. By exhibiting confidence, strength, and a cooperative soul, you rouse others to take part in certain and useful systems administration rehearses.

By integrating these positive initiative standards into systems administration endeavors, experts can make an organization portrayed by realness, sympathy, correspondence, and persistent development. This approach enhances proficient connections as well as adds to long haul achievement and satisfaction.

Chapter Twenty

"Initiative Heritage: Molding A Positive Effect For People In The future"

Initiative heritage includes purposefully forming a positive effect that stretches out past one's nearby residency, leaving an enduring impact on people in the future. It rises above transient accomplishments, zeroing in on the persevering through values, culture, and commitments a pioneer gives to their association and the more extensive local area.

At its center, initiative heritage is tied in with developing a positive and maintainable hierarchical culture. Pioneers who focus on moral practices, inclusivity, and a feeling of direction make an establishment that reverberates with people in the future. By imparting these qualities, they add to the advancement of mindful, caring, and ground breaking pioneers.

Positive initiative inheritance additionally includes mentorship and information sharing. Pioneers who put resources into fostering the abilities and initiative capability of others add to a pipeline of fit and engaged people. This mentorship cultivates a culture of consistent learning and development, guaranteeing that the positive effect perseveres through progressive ages of pioneers.

Charity and local area commitment are necessary parts of an initiative inheritance. Pioneers who effectively add to local area government assistance and social causes leave a positive engraving on the world past their hierarchical domain. This obligation to having an effect turns out to be important for the pioneer's heritage, moving others to add to everyone's benefit.

Eventually, initiative inheritance is an intentional and cognizant work to shape a positive effect that rises above the current second. It includes imparting values, encouraging development, and adding to the prosperity of both the association and the more extensive local area, making an enduring and positive impact for people in the future.

Key Idea; Investigating how a positive administration mentality adds to an enduring heritage in the business world.

A positive administration mentality is instrumental in forming an enduring heritage in the business world, adding to supported achievement and effect over the long haul. This is the way such an outlook assumes a significant part:

1. Values-Driven Leadership:

Positive pioneers focus on values that line up with moral practices, respectability, and social obligation. By reliably exhibiting and building up these qualities, they make a hierarchical culture that perseveres past their residency, framing the establishment for a positive inheritance.

2. Inspiring And Engaging Teams:

Positive pioneers motivate and enable their groups. By encouraging a culture of trust, cooperation, and inclusivity, they add to the improvement of a spurred and connected with labor force. This strengthening prompts quick accomplishment as well as guarantees a tradition of skilled and spurred experts.

3. Strategic Choice Making:

A positive initiative mentality includes key dynamic that thinks about long haul suggestions. Pioneers who gauge the effect of their choices on the association's future add to a tradition of strength and flexibility, situating the business for supported achievement.

4. Innovation And Adaptability:

Inspiration supports development and flexibility. Pioneers who embrace change and energize a culture of imagination leave a tradition of consistent improvement. This ground breaking approach positions the association to flourish in advancing business scenes.

5. Mentorship And Progression Planning:

Positive pioneers put resources into mentorship and progression arranging. By fostering the abilities and initiative capability of others, they make a tradition of able and enabled people who can convey the association forward.

6. Customer-Driven Approach:

Positive pioneers focus on a client driven approach. By cultivating a culture that values consumer loyalty and input, they leave a tradition of client faithfulness and supported business connections.

7. Adherence To Corporate Social Obligation (CSR):

Embracing corporate social obligation is a sign of positive initiative. Pioneers who coordinate CSR into the business methodology leave a tradition of contributing decidedly to society, upgrading the organization's standing and leaving an enduring effect past monetary achievement.

<u>Conclusion</u>

In the end pages of "Careful Initiative: Creating Your Prosperity Through a Positive Authority Mentality," our process arrives at its zenith, encapsulating the pith of "Exploring Difficulties, Motivating Groups."

This complete aide isn't simply an assortment of techniques; a compass explores the nuanced scene of authority in the cutting edge business world.

From the careful route of difficulties to the craft of motivating groups, every section unfurls as a plan for molding a positive initiative outlook.

The resonating subject is clear: achievement isn't only an objective yet a nonstop excursion powered by care, versatility, and a promise to cultivating aggregate development.

As you consider the bits of knowledge shared, may you incorporate the significance of a positive initiative mentality. It's about private accomplishment as well as about the significant effect you can have in groups and associations. Administration, as portrayed in these pages, is a workmanship — a nonstop creating of progress from a perspective of care, sympathy, and motivation.

The excursion doesn't end with the end of this book; rather, it stretches out into the texture of your initiative methodology.

May you convey forward the standards of careful authority, exploring difficulties with certainty, and motivating groups for getting through progress. As you step into the unique scene of the cutting edge business world, may your initiative be set apart by energy, strength, and a pledge to molding an enduring example of overcoming adversity.